INTERPRETERS SUPPORTING INTERPRETERS

*A team of sign language interpreters
collaborating to make the field
a better place for all through mentoring*

Interpreters Supporting Interpreters © CORE Interpreters, 2020
Developed by Caitlin Ramsey Wolford and Katherine Perchik
Edited by June Lucarotti
Book design by HR Hegnauer

Paperback ISBN: 978-0-578-78326-0
eBook ISBN: 978-0-578-78343-7

CORE Interpreters LLC exists to provide a space for sign language interpreters to grow their skills and develop a network among other interpreters through mentorship, community-based learning, and partnering with the Deaf community.

CONTENTS

1 · The Program

19 · Colleague Advancement

41 · Outreach

57 · Resources

67 · Ethics

83 · Call to Action

THE PROGRAM

WHY MENTORSHIP?

Interpreting is a human, service-oriented, skill-based practitioner field. Interpreters committed to furthering the field must focus their attention on developing the following:

- More inclusive and supportive workplaces
- A variety of opportunities for skill development
- Deeper engagement by partnering with local communities
- Stronger leadership to support the next generation of interpreters

The goal of a mentorship is to improve personal and professional outcomes while creating a cultural shift in the interpreting field.

WHY CORE?

The CORE Program was established with the purpose of enhancing the field of interpreting by creating a collaborative space for interpreters to support one another. We value your time and your commitment to this aspiration.

During your CORE experience we want to provide you with the necessary tools and information to make this a successful experience. The CORE book is one such tool. Our Team has created this resource, which is both a curriculum guide and workbook, in order to maximize your mentoring experience while in the CORE Program.

Communication and commitment are key to making this a positive experience for all involved. Please be sure to carefully read the following responsibilities and tips provided below in order to make your experience with CORE a fulfilling one.

What lessons from colleagues and the Deaf community do you still carry with you today?

As you consider these questions, think also of the interpreters who would include you on a list of people who supported their development. Would your name be included in many lists? What lessons do you want to pass on?

HELICOPTER PHENOMENA

The CORE Program aims to facilitate the transfer of knowledge from one generation to the next. As a field, interpreters must look inward to support the growth of the next generation. As one generation begins exiting the workforce, their institutional knowledge about the interpreting field will leave with them, this is why mentorship is key.

CORE is a unique mentorship experience because of the structure and roles each person has in the Program. CORE believes in facilitating the transfer of knowledge across generations and providing support through multiple channels. Since the establishment of CORE in 2017, we have seen hundreds of interpreters successfully complete the CORE Program and reap the benefits of the CORE support structure. Below is a visualization of this structure:

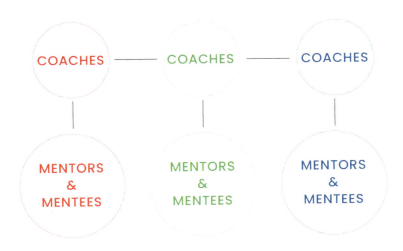

During our Kickoff Events which mark the beginning of each new CORE Cycle, we use the metaphor of a helicopter to explain the narrative of mentorship in the interpreting field. Those experienced interpreters who are in our proverbial helicopter have to throw out a rope to guide and support the generation coming behind them. This is where the role of the Coach comes into play. Often interpreters with institutional knowledge, a strong network, and deeper understanding of the interpreting field are not as available to early career interpreters or interpreters who want to become a Mentor. Coaches are the people with the teaching experience, knowledge, and support but they often lack the necessary time to impart their wisdom to each individual person. This is why in the CORE Program we pair Coaches together to lead a Team of interpreters.

Alongside the Coaches, each Team consists of several Mentor-Mentee pairs. The goal of CORE is to encourage early career interpreters by assigning them a Mentor to work with one-on-one. Mentees are paired with Mentors based on areas they wish to develop, personality, and whatever other criteria the CORE Match Team uses. By using this structure, the Mentees are paired directly with one Mentor who is invested in their development, while at the same time, those Mentees can tap into the larger network of their two Coaches and the entire CORE Team.

Mentors are often interpreters who are either new to mentoring or who have mentored for several years and wish to continue to invest in one-on-one relationships with Mentees. CORE recognizes that Mentors are also busy, which is why the above model was designed to provide additional support from the Coaches and the extended CORE Team. Mentors are really the rope that connects the Mentees on the ground to the Coaches in the helicopter.

CORE envisions the trade off in this way: Mentees receive the necessary support in order to be successful in the field of interpreting; Mentors are able to sharpen their mentorship skills; Coaches further their knowledge of mentorship by working alongside their peers. CORE believes every interpreter involved possesses beneficial knowledge to share.

THE MISSION

Interpreters Supporting Interpreters

THE MEANING

COLLEAGUE ADVANCEMENT
Mentoring for everyone

OUTREACH
Sharing the knowledge

RESOURCES
Equipping interpreters

ETHICS
Principled approach to interpreting

COLLEAGUE ADVANCEMENT
Mentoring for everyone

As a skill based practitioner field, sign language interpreters must continue to learn how to improve interpersonal and intrapersonal skills. Interpreters are engaged in an on-going journey learning new information about the interpreting field. The context and setting of an interpreter's job may change daily. CORE believes each interpreter should have a support system in place to support not only individual growth, but the collective growth of the whole CORE Team. The CORE model has a built-in network of interpreters and a safety net for Mentors who are new to mentoring. With a three tiered approach, two Coaches work alongside one another while mentoring several pairs of Mentors and Mentees.

OUTREACH
Sharing the knowledge

CORE provides opportunities for interpreters to work alongside fellow practitioners in teaming situations through pro bono assignments within the community. This allows interpreters to reflect the dynamic nature of teaming and gives them the chance to share feedback with colleagues in a safe environment. The shared experience of being in the CORE Program gives both interpreters a foundation of relationship, context, and a support system.

RESOURCES
Equipping interpreters

While in the CORE Program, interpreters are able to attend professional development workshops and events hosted by CORE. Along with the CORE curriculum in this workbook, access to the network of interpreters involved with CORE in its respective localities is crucial to individual development. With several Chapters across the United States, interpreters involved with the CORE Program also gain the unique ability to join a national network of CORE interpreters.

ETHICS
Principled approach to interpreting

Since the establishment of CORE in 2017, the Deaf community and sign language interpreting community have partnered together to bring this CORE Program to fruition. CORE was founded on the belief that sign language interpreters must work in parallel with the Deaf community at large. CORE accomplishes this mission by involving Deaf community members in various roles within the CORE Program and through providing pro bono interpreting services within local communities.

ABOUT THE MENTORSHIP PROGRAM

Our Program spans a six month period during which two interpreters are placed together by the Match Team. We have a few requirements for Mentor and Mentee pairs which are outlined in further detail below.

- Team interpreting a minimum of two pro bono jobs vetted by CORE

- Meeting a minimum of once a month to discuss skill development

- Virtually connecting at minimum once a month to check-in

- Attending the CORE Kickoff Event as well as the CORE Completion Event

- Attending three CORE workshops (CEUs offered for free)

Our CORE Team recognizes the need for supporting one another as we develop side-by-side. Whether you are an experienced Mentor with decades of teaching experience or an early career interpreter, we believe each member of this Program has something unique to offer. Our Program's safety net approach means that if a Mentor and Mentee pair needs support or resources, the two assigned Coaches for their Team can provide an extra layer of guidance. Each Team will have virtual or in person meetings which provides Mentors and Mentees with an opportunity to learn from others and grow their network.

Giving back to the Deaf community is extremely important. Each Mentor and Mentee pair is required to work a minimum of two pro bono assignments while in the CORE Program. While CORE maintains a list of potential pro bono opportunities for each pair to choose from each Cycle, we will also permit Mentors and Mentees to find their own pro bono opportunities. We expect all Mentors and Mentees to use their own discretion in determining if the pro bono assignment is an appropriate match for the skill level of both interpreters, as well as ethically sound.

The purpose of the CORE Checklist is to provide Mentors and Mentees with a standard set of expectations to guide their mentorship experience while in the CORE Program. Each month of the Cycle has a theme on which Mentors and Mentees should focus. We have also provided very specific actionable items Mentors and Mentees must complete each month. Items in the Checklist below serve as a starting point for Mentors and Mentees, however, the CORE Team does encourage each Mentor and Mentee pair to tailor their mentorship experience to fit their goals, professional relationship, and schedule.

CHECKLIST

MONTH 1

Relationship
- Complete Manifesto
- Clarify standard expectations for mentoring relationship
- Communicate with Coaches
- Attend Kickoff

MONTH 2

Target Skills
- Begin to identify two pro bono opportunities
- List specific structure to tackle skills
- Complete video interpreting work to share
- Discuss preferences for feedback
- Attend CORE Event

MONTH 3

Skill Development
- Revisit the Manifesto for revisions
- Complete video interpreting work to share
- Provide feedback on video interpreting work
- Contact Coaches with update on progress
- Attend CORE Event

MONTH 4
Progression of Skill
- Revisit Manifesto to discuss progress
- Complete video interpreting work to share
- Provide feedback on video interpreting work
- Completed at least one pro bono assignment
- Attend CORE Event

MONTH 5
Transformation of Skill
- Contact Coaches with update on progress
- Complete video interpreting work to share
- Provide feedback on video work
- Reflect on Manifesto
- Attend CORE Event

MONTH 6
Assessment & Next Steps
- Strategize three new goals for the Mentee
- Revisit CORE Career Map to plan next steps
- Complete CORE survey
- Report number of pro bono hours completed
- Attend CORE Completion Event

MANIFESTO

The CORE Manifesto is a living and breathing document that we ask each Mentor and Mentee pair to devise to provide structure to their time working together. Each pair creates their own Manifesto which both Coaches will then review for edits or clarifications. Following approval by the Coaches, the pair will submit the signed Manifesto to their CORE Chapter Organizer and Coaches. During the Cycle, if necessary, Mentors and Mentees may make edits to their Manifesto, making sure to inform their Coaches of the revisions.

The Manifesto should answer the following questions:

Contribution

- What is the legacy you want to leave behind in the field?

- What do you want to accomplish in this Program?

- How can you support other interpreters in this Program?

- What will be the result of your involvement with this Program?

- How can pairs work together for more effective communication?

Actions

- What are the current resources you have to offer in your toolkit?

- How can you prioritize what you want to accomplish?

- If you were able to accomplish anything without limitations, what would it be?

- What is one efficient approach to communication that you can implement using technology?

Results

- How will you measure success?

- Who can keep you accountable to your goals?

- What is your next immediate step to achieve your goal?

- How often can you check in with one another?

MANIFESTO
Interpreters Supporting Interpreters

This contract serves as an agreement between _____ and _____ to commit to this growth experience together. Our goals as Mentee and Mentor have been outlined to fit the specific needs of our working relationship. We commit to the expectations and objectives below. We commit to adhere to this Manifesto to the best of our abilities during our participation in this CORE Cycle.

We have agreed to focus on the following goals/objectives for the Mentee's development throughout this growth experience:

-
-
-

We have discussed expectations and protocols by which we will work together in order to complete the Checklist during the six-month mentorship. To ensure that our relationship is a fulfilling experience for both of us, we agree to abide by the following expectations:

-
-
-

Mentor signature _____ Date _____

Mentee signature _____ Date _____

Congratulations! Enjoy!

COLLEAGUE ADVANCEMENT

Mentoring for everyone

Mentorship is crucial for development and a beautiful expression of what can happen when colleagues support one another with humility and respect. Many tenured interpreters can think back on their time in the field and name several interpreters who supported them along the way. Interpreting is a difficult field requiring a support system and a community of people who understand the nuances associated with being an interpreter.

- **If you are a Mentee in CORE**
  What do you believe are the three most important qualities for a Mentee in a Mentor-Mentee relationship?

- **If you are a Mentor in CORE**
  What qualities did previous Mentors teach you that were successful in your Mentor-Mentee relationships?

- **If you are a Coach in CORE**
  How can you leverage a collaborative environment to create a positive mentorship experience?

CORE STRUCTURE
Safety net approach

Each participant in the CORE Program plays an important part in creating a safe place for everyone to grow. Below are the benefits and responsibilities for each role within the CORE Program. Additionally, each interpreter who is an RID certified or associate member is eligible to earn 1.2 Continuing Education Units (CEUs) by attending the three CORE workshops hosted each Cycle.

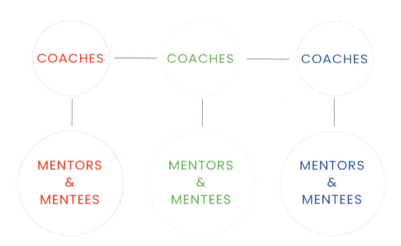

Coaches
- Support one entire Team
- Partner with another Coach
- Present workshops for Cycle
- Access to workshops in Cycle
- Share institutional knowledge
- CORE Booklet

Mentors
- Support one Mentee
- Supported by two Coaches
- Access to workshops in Cycle
- Develop mentorship skills
- Develop stronger reputation
- CORE Booklet

Mentees
- Supported by one Mentor
- Supported by two Coaches
- Access to workshops in Cycle
- Expand professional network
- Develop brand
- Develop reputation
- Develop interpreting skills
- CORE Booklet

TIPS FOR COACHES
Responsibilities in providing support

Communication
- Correspond within the Team
- Manage Team morale
- Maintain strong connections with each Mentor and Mentee pair

Community
- Collaborate with local interpreters in your network
- Connect Mentors and Mentees to the larger CORE Program
- Facilitating collective dialogue among your Team

Leading
- Set an example with ethical decision-making
- Empower interpreters to be their authentic selves
- Educate yourself and others on different cultural competencies

Resource
- Impart institutional knowledge, lessons learned, and experiences that should never be forgotten
- Share tips and tricks about interpreting, running a business, and more
- Provide additional materials to the interpreters based on their goals

Confidence
- Believe in capabilities, not only in your ability to further the CORE mission but in your ability to provide support

How can you support long-term growth with interpreters on your Team?

What kind of legacy will you leave for the field?

What leadership skills do you have?

How do you build community?

What is your approach to mentoring?

What resources do you have to offer your Team?

TIPS FOR MENTORS
Mentor guidance

Opportunities
- Team interpreting
- Work together on minimum of two pro bono assignments
- Join workshops to personally develop and to support those in attendance at the workshop
- Clearly define your goals for Mentor/Mentee relationship
- Prepare for each meeting by brainstorming skill development activities for Mentee

Active Listening
- Give thoughtful and specific feedback
- Rather than diagnosing, listen to the Mentee
- Accept feedback once ready to hear it
- Allow time to process feedback
- Reflective practice
- Take notes

Transparency
- Be clear about personal and professional boundaries
- Be open about concerns and limitations
- Be honest when you don't know the answer
- Be real about your personal experiences

Safety
- Create an ethical cone of silence within your Mentor-Mentee relationship
- Build a relationship with your Mentee that is dependent upon trust

Gain and Provide Insight
- Engage in mutually beneficial professional relationship by sharing perspectives
- Learn how to improve upon your mentoring skills from Coaches with decades of experience
- Educate yourself on different cultural competencies
- Provide feedback to CORE regarding your experience

Notes

Consider your own positive mentoring experiences in the past.
How can you incorporate those into this Program?

How can you be more of an active listener?

What are you wanting to improve in regards to your mentoring skills?

How can you incorporate reflective practice into mentoring?

What boundaries do you need to set personally regarding your schedule?

How do you prefer to communicate with a Mentee?

TIPS FOR MENTEES
Mentee motivation

Set Goals
- Be specific
- List the skills you want to target while in CORE Cycle
- Monitor your progress
- Provide measurable and achievable goals using a structured framework

Communication
- While in CORE take initiative to schedule meetings with your Mentor
- Discover preferences and approaches to communication
- Discuss communication styles and schedules with a foundation of mutual understanding
- Provide consistency and respond during both in-person and virtual meetings
- Refer to Checklist on a monthly basis

Appreciation
- Celebrate the growth and accomplishments of colleagues
- Respect professional boundaries and be honest about your needs
- Express gratitude for someone supporting your career
- Foster a collaborative work environment by supporting the successes of other colleagues

Retrospection
- Remember you are on a learning curve; it takes time to build skill sets
- Consider your starting point within CORE
- Document the change you want to see while in the Program
- Renegotiate needs throughout the Cycle if necessary

Feedback
- Willingness to be open
- Receiving feedback can cause feelings of discomfort or embarrassment
- Be honest about how you feel
- Approach feedback, both in receiving and delivering, with authenticity

Notes

What skills or knowledge can you offer to your Team?

What do you want to get out of this Program?

What skills do you want to improve?

What resources do you currently use to improve your skills?

How do you prefer to communicate with a Mentor?

What was successful or not successful about
your previous experiences with mentors?

MENTORING PHILOSOPHIES
Not one size fits all

Direct Feedback - *preferences*
Communicates clearly by receiving and giving honest feedback. Provides support on specific aspects of work that are either diagnostic or relational. Interpersonal and intrapersonal skills can be addressed head-on rather than after they become ingrained habits. Interpreters must be mentally prepared for this discussion and be willing to develop a career map to achieve tangible results to show progress.

Peer to Peer - *relationships*
Works together to foster a collaborative professional relationship that inspires discussion between two interpreters with similar work experiences and backgrounds. Often interpreters working alongside one another in daily teaming assignments can use this approach to support one another. Encourages mutuality and morale support among peers.

Supervision - *oversight*
Maintains oversight of the interpreting process and career of another interpreter. Ensures the correct processes and necessary supports are provided for an early career interpreter.

Collective Dialogue - *community of practice*
> Creates an environment for different ideas to surface while considering potential frameworks for perceiving the world dependent upon lived experiences. Includes interpreting theories and models for how to improve real-time decision making for future assignments. Allows for innovative thinking and problem-solving.

Reflective Practice - *reframe*
> Uses personal experiences as a frame of reference for discussion and best practices. This approach provides greater awareness of the interpreting process, situational awareness, and demonstrates introspective thinking and self analysis.

TOPICS FOR DISCUSSION

When mentoring, there are many approaches to discussing the interpreting field. Consider the ideas below as potential strategies for initiating relevant, professional, and ethical conversations between practicing interpreters. Exchanging tricks of the trade or tools to add to one's toolbox can be beneficial when the unexpected happens.

Overcoming the Challenges
Discuss lessons learned throughout your career. Use the Ethical Scenarios available in the CORE Resource Library to discuss potential scenarios an interpreter may experience while on an assignment.

Local Insights
Share beneficial tips for navigating the local interpreting and Deaf communities. This may include information about local interpreting agencies along with pros and cons for each and recommendations for networking opportunities.

Develop Scripts
Create a schema for responding to frequent interpreting scenarios where interpreters must advocate for themselves.

Ingredients for Success
Dialogue about professional attire, punctuality, ethical decision-making, and screening which assignments are a suitable match for ones' skill level and experience.

Resume Building
Provide feedback on format, clarity, syntax, and content. Use the CORE Resume Template which can be found in the CORE Resource Library on the CORE Website, as a foundation for creating an updated resume. Discuss how to expand upon current or future opportunities. Also, utilize the Resources section of this book to help guide you in building your resume.

Specializing
Discuss a variety of potential work settings, as well as personal interests and/or hobbies, which could influence interpreter suitability.

Notes

AUTHENTICITY

Prior to launching a career, there are common questions to which interpreters need answers. Mentorship is most successful when both the Mentor and Mentee are interested and open to learning authentically from one another and addressing those questions. Create a safe and open space for one another built on trust, respect, and appreciation of lived experiences.

Within this mutually created, sacred space of mentorship, interpreters are able to actively engage from a position of truthfulness and understanding. This space can foster a dialogue between an interpreter with decades of experience and an early career interpreter, in which both can provide beneficial insights from their unique lenses. Each person adds value to the mentorship experience.

Utilize the space below to brainstorm discussion topics and questions that will lead to the development of a sacred space of mentorship:

INTERSECTIONAL IDENTITIES

Interpreters work with a variety of people who come from different backgrounds, experiences, races, and cultures. It is important for interpreters to educate themselves on various identities, and how these may show up while working and mentoring.

When researching or learning about specific communities, it is crucial to learn from those who identify as members of those communities. Note that the two lists below are not exhaustive or complete, but can be used as a way of educating yourself.

Communities to Educate Yourself

- Black
- Indigenous
- People of Color (POC)
- Hispanic
- Children of Deaf Adults (CODA)
- LGBTQIA+
- Judaism
- Muslim
- Buddhism
- DeafBlind
- Neurodiversity
- Latino

Terminology to Educate Yourself

- Microaggressions
- Ableism
- Audism
- Cultural appropriation
- Gender expression
- Internalized oppression
- Prejudice
- Anti-racist
- Homophobia
- Religious oppression
- Privilege
- Racial profiling
- Gender identity
- Ethnocentrism
- Empathy

As you navigate the world and the interpreting profession, you will find that no list can address every unique cultural identity or term. The lists above are just the beginning of what should be a continual journey of self-guided research. The goal is to learn about communities, cultures, beliefs, and ideas different from your own.

OUTREACH

Sharing the knowledge

When establishing an interpreting career, creating a clear brand and business model is essential for your reputation. A brand or business model should reflect an interpreter's commitment to developing a deep understanding of the profession and the Deaf experience.

By engaging in relationships with and studying content created by Deaf people and interpreters who are considered pillars in the field, interpreters are developing their brand into one that is recognized and trusted throughout the community, thus preparing themselves to carry on institutional knowledge to the next generation of practitioners. Through this process, interpreters gain an understanding of the lived experiences of Deaf people — knowledge that can guide an interpreter's decisions and perspectives as they grow their careers.

- **If you are a Mentee in CORE**
  What are the three qualities you want to be known for within the Deaf community?

- **If you are a Mentor in CORE**
  How can this CORE mentoring experience elevate your reputation and brand?

- **If you are a Coach in CORE**
  How can you give feedback to Mentors and Mentees about their reputation and brand?

BRANDING
Tips for a successful career

Introspective Analysis
- Think about how your journey led you to where you stand in the Deaf community, to whom do you owe a debt of gratitude
- Consider specialties you wish to pursue in your work
- Be open to receiving and incorporating feedback from your peers and the community
- Engage in mentoring relationships as a form of skill development and network building
- Think of the long term effect you would like to have on the overall interpreting field
- Set goals, both long term and short term, to guide your career
- Create an actionable plan to achieve these goals (i.e.: career map) and revisit it often

Start-Up Business
- Consider whether or not you would like to establish a Limited Liability Corporation
- Create an Employer Identification Number (EIN) with the Internal Revenue Service (IRS)
- Consider working with a professional tax preparer or Certified Professional Accountant (CPA)
- Plan for retirement early on in your career and intentionally allocate funds toward retirement

Branding Assets
- Create business cards listing your preferred contact information and up-to-date credentials
- Develop a professional resume and update it regularly
- Ensure that all of your branding assets, including resume, terms and conditions, and business cards, are clear and consistent in formatting
- Consider creating a website or e-portfolio

Online Presence
- Be intentional about designing your social media presence to reflect your specialized interests
- Be aware of your social media following and how they will receive any content you share
- Research how you can craft your online presence into a marketing platform

Notes

CREATING YOUR BRAND

As sole proprietors, it is essential for interpreters to develop and maintain ongoing working relationships within their communities. One way to do so is through brand management. Brand management when operating any business is essential for growth and longevity in the field. There are several approaches to brand development.

For example, clear messaging through a standardized business name, logo, license, and website can help shape your professional reputation. Additionally, consistent messaging to your audience and being open to feedback can be essential in maintaining this reputation.

Maintaining a brand both in promotional materials and in business practices when working within the Deaf community can help others, especially those within the Deaf and interpreting communities, recognize that you, as an interpreter stand for quality.

Research the brands of local interpreters and interpreters nationwide that you can learn from. Are there any features that you could see incorporating into your own personal brand?

INTRAPERSONAL & INTERPERSONAL SKILLS

While interpreters can develop a reputation through their branding, they maintain it through every interaction they have with clients, teams, agency representatives, etc, while on the job. In order to ensure they are presenting themselves in a way that reflects their brand and values, interpreters must be cognizant of their interpersonal and intrapersonal skills. As interpreters, we must consider how both our lived experiences and interpreting skills are intertwined with our work and how we engage with consumers on the receiving end of our interpretations.

INTRAPERSONAL SKILLS

In addition to being communication facilitators, interpreters are often called upon to exercise the "soft" skills of cultural mediation. In a setting where both parties come from different cultural backgrounds, it is up to the interpreter to have an understanding and appreciation of both in order to mediate any conflicts or misunderstandings that may arise during an interpretation. This is where interpreters call upon their intrapersonal skills.

Interpreters must be open to learning about others' lived experiences, especially when it comes to those with backgrounds different from their own. Along with diverse backgrounds come a variety of social cues. Social cues, while subtle, often speak volumes. Interpreters must be able to pick up on this nuanced layer of communication as it has the potential to impact an interpreted situation.

Communication styles and dynamics also play a role in teaming. Interpreters must be aware of and able to adjust their own communication style depending on who they are working with and what that relationship looks like. This, combined with a willingness to engage in the exchange of feedback, will enhance the collaboration between a team.

Along with the lived experience of others, interpreters must be aware of who they are as dynamic and multifaceted individuals. Through introspective work, interpreters can develop an awareness of their own privilege, worldview, personality traits, biases, and preferences. With this understanding, interpreters can then acknowledge how all of this has the potential to show up in their work and take steps to prevent it from influencing an interpreted exchange or at least be aware of the influence and engage in dialogue and modification.

Finally, while these examples are not exhaustive, a professional interpreter must be organized. Punctuality and other basic organizational skills are vital in the success and longevity of one's career.

Questions to consider:

- How do you handle time management and being punctual?

- Are you aware of your own personality traits that could have an impact on the work?

- Do you have any pet-peeves and how do you manage those on a job?

- Do you have effective and adaptable communication strategies?

- Are you willing to collaborate with other interpreters and consumers on the job?

- Are you organized in both your personal life and professional life?

- Do you have the ability to pick up on social cues?

- Do you respect cultural norms of other ethnicities? Are you educated about other cultures?

- What is your role in cultural mediation on the job?

- Can you put your personal biases aside when on a job?

- Do you have an appreciation for everyone's unique lived experiences and backgrounds?

- Do you acknowledge your privilege(s) and the role it plays in various settings?

INTERPERSONAL SKILLS

Interpreters of any length of experience understand that this line of work is nuanced and complex. Every aspect of the work is centered around interactions with other people, whether it be a team interpreter, a client, whether Deaf or hearing, or any of the multitudes of individuals we come in contact with before, during, and after assignments. Interpersonal skills are those needed to manage these interactions.

When it comes to working with a team, interpreters must be comfortable with the concept of feeding information to one another. Every interpreter at some point or another will need to prompt, cue, or feed relevant information to a team interpreter; this may be in the form of receiving a feed or transmitting a feed to your team. Recognizing the need for clarification or support and being able to act on those needs is an essential interpersonal skill. It is absolutely crucial to identify areas where you typically struggle, such as fingerspelled words, numbers, technical jargon, etc. Being able to convey this information to your team is the first step in establishing successful feeding experience.

If an interpreter is working solo, they must be able to ask clients for clarification effectively when they notice potential misunderstandings or omissions in their work. All of this helps to enhance one of the most essential "hard" skills for an interpreter: producing a conceptually and linguistically accurate message. Clear production coupled with natural sounding prosody can make an interpreter's output that much more comprehensible for all clients. Additionally, interpreters must possess familiarity with the linguistic needs and signing/speaking styles of clients as well as a basic understanding of the content they are interpreting. Being culturally competent and humble when working alongside various Deaf consumers from different backgrounds is critical when interpreting.

These skills require years of dedicated learning and skill development. Interpreters, by entering this field, must recognize that they are committing themselves to a life of learning. They must continuously engage in measurable skill development and diagnostic work, both independently and alongside colleagues and other members of the field.

Questions to consider:

- Do you know the regional signs specific to your locality?

- What are approaches to providing a feed to a team?

- Do you know how to receive feeds efficiently from a team?

- Do you know how to effectively ask for clarification from a consumer?

- How do you communicate with your interpreting team?

- How do you explain your areas of strength while interpreting?

- How do you explain your areas of weakness while interpreting?

BIASES & TRANSPARENCY

As a human, we all have our own personal biases and beliefs. Interpreters working with a variety of people must ask themselves hard questions about what we believe or why we feel a certain way. Becoming aware of your own beliefs by digging deep to discover your own biases will better equip you to take on the role of a third party communication facilitator in different settings. As interpreters, we witness the Deaf community in various life situations, and it is important to check our own internal biases and beliefs prior to accepting an assignment.

When in a Mentor-Mentee relationship, each person brings their own life experiences and beliefs. Respect is the foundational quality of every good relationship, including that of the Mentor-Mentee. When two people from different backgrounds come together, in any form, it requires introspection and the asking of hard questions by both parties. Put your humanity first, and the role of interpreter second. As you work through a difficult situation, ask yourself the questions below to guide you in the process of analyzing your own beliefs, bigotries, and feelings. Lead yourself to a place where you are more transparent with your complex, multifaceted self.

Questions to consider:

- Why do I believe what I believe?

- Who taught me to feel this way about this situation?

- What am I not seeing, that others are seeing?

- How can I become more educated on this topic?

- Why did that action hurt my feelings?

- How can I become more aware of my own biases?

SCHEDULERS

Interpreters often work as subcontractors or with larger interpreting agencies both locally and nationally. Since interpreting depends heavily on interactive relationships with multiple parties, interpreters must learn how to be strong communicators. One relationship which is especially important is that of the interpreter and the agency scheduler or coordinator. It is essential that interpreters maintain a connection with schedulers through clear and consistent communication. Such communication may look like the following:

- Notifying schedulers of time off requests as far in advance as possible (i.e. vacations, medical appointments, family reunions, house repairs, etc.)
- Responding to emails with gratitude and clarity
- Being clear about which assignments match your skill set and forthcoming when you might be feeling overwhelmed
- Notifying schedulers of on-the-job changes (i.e. go beyond the scheduled time, client is a no show, etc.)
- Recognizing that prep information about an assignment may be limited or scarce
- Appreciating that schedulers are working to provide support to multiple parties and exercising patience with them in your responses

List the schedulers in your network and reach out to show them some appreciation for their hard work:

RESOURCES

Equipping interpreters

An interpreter toolkit can be very beneficial when starting off a career. One's toolkit can be anything from a well-packed bag for freelance days, to a cohesive long-term financial plan, to a strong resumé. The resources provided by CORE in this chapter are tangible actions that interpreters can take to build this toolkit and, in turn, improve their interpreting work and long-term career. In addition to those provided by CORE, there are many online resources and books about interpreting which we also encourage you to utilize to expand your knowledge.

- **If you are a Mentee in CORE**
  What tools or resources do you think you need to enhance your development?

- **If you are a Mentor in CORE**
  What tools or resources have you implemented in your professional life that have benefited your career?

- **If you are a Coach in CORE**
  How have you incorporated tools and resources that have benefited the longevity of your career and how can you share these resources with your Team?

INTERPRETER'S BACKPACK

When a job depends on having your hands free but not having an assigned office the majority of the time, it is helpful to have a way to carry your personal items. Given that interpreters are often "on-the-go," it is essential to find a backpack or other bag that is large enough to hold everything you need while still being ergonomically designed to prevent any pain or injury. Another consideration is the security or screening protocols you will be expected to follow while on an assignment. Keep this in mind as you pack your bag for the day.

Here are some common items that interpreters should consider carrying with them to assignments:

Electronics
- Phone and charger
- Laptop/tablet and charger
- Head phones
- Back-up charger
- Personal hotspot for internet access
- Planner (digital)

Records
- Driver's license
- Assignment-specific badges
- Notebook or paper for teaming notes
- Physical planner or agenda

Personal Items
- Prescription medications
- Pain medications (Tylenol, Aspirin, Ibuprofen, etc.)
- Band-aids
- Vitamin C supplements
- Antibacterial hand wipes
- Gel or spray hand sanitizer
- Tissues
- Cough drops
- Mints or gum
- Tidy and easily accessible snacks
- Reusable water bottle
- Cash for on-site cafeterias or vending machines

RESUME SUPPORT

Maintaining a quality resumé and updating it frequently is important for your career development. Doing so can help you identify and pursue new opportunities. Below are a few items to keep in mind while creating and updating your resumé. Ask another interpreter to proofread its content for confidentiality, grammar, and overall format.

Confidentiality
- Do not list specific clientele or locations
- Keep information general rather than specific
  (ie: secondary education, higher education, emergency room, etc)

Ethics
- Ensure the time frame for each work experience is accurate
- Certifications listed

Experience
- Organize positions in chronological order
- Organize positions held simultaneously by relevance
- Include previous jobs if they are relevant to your current career

Appearance
- Maintain clear, consistent formatting between resumé, terms and conditions, and other professional materials
- Work with a proofreader to review grammar, spelling, and clarity

Professionalism
- Consider creating a professional email address separate from your personal email address
- Include a minimum of three references, including a member of the Deaf community who can vouch for your skillset and professionalism and two certified interpreters
- Get permission before including someone as a reference and ask their preferred contact method
- Show appreciation for your references and keep them updated on your career moves
- Personal contact information

Notes

BUDGETING

Most interpreters work as independent contractors, therefore, it is our responsibility to plan for tax season, long-term/short-term savings, and retirement. Work is not always consistent, so it is important interpreters keep an accurate budget. This will help ensure they are able to meet all financial obligations. Here are some steps you can incorporate into your financial journey to provide you a sense of control and peace of mind.

STEP 1
Register for budget application

With various online and mobile applications ranging in price from free to just a few dollars a month, there are numerous ways to approach organizing your spending and earning. Find a system that works for you. Consider such functionality as the ability to track bills and payments received and remitted and the option to categorize personal or business related expenses.

STEP 2
Action items

Create categories to track daily, weekly, monthly, and yearly expenses. Predictable, ongoing expenses such as rent or mortgages, retirement contributions, utility bills, and loan payments should be automated. Miscellaneous, one-off, or infrequent payments should be recorded and categorized accordingly.

STEP 3
Analyze your recurring and miscellaneous expenses

Most electronic applications have algorithms and statistical graphs to summarize outputs and inputs. Identify spending habits and monthly recurring payments and compare this to hours worked and payments received.

STEP 4
Implement system

Begin using the new electronic application to track each input and output. Determine if the system is adequate for daily needs. Double check expenses paid versus earnings.

STEP 5
Evaluate and decide

Proceed with expenditures, savings account contributions and accepting and declining assignments with the knowledge of a personal budget and the ability to make informed decisions about expenses and work assignments based on actual numbers.

SELF CARE

As communication facilitators, interpreters are constantly depicting other people's personalities and actions. With such a unique opportunity to see the world from so many perspectives, interpreters often leave assignments with the knowledge of others' lived experiences, both positive and negative. In order to prevent burnout from potential vicarious trauma, consider a self-care routine which includes your mental and physical health. Interpreters must keep their work confidential which may make finding an outlet to express on-the-job trauma more difficult. However, there are many ways to practice self care while simultaneously maintaining confidentiality. Below are a few strategies for addressing mental and physical health.

MENTAL HEALTH

Actions
- Therapy
- Find a third party to listen and provide advice
- Learn and employ tools to manage experiences
- Journaling
- Practice positive self talk
- Create a list of things you are grateful for
- Reflect on your lived experiences
- Set goals for personal growth

Benefits
- Vicarious trauma support
- Validation of experiences
- Opportunity for confidential sharing
- Adopt a growth-mindset
- Develop introspective thinking skills

Notes

PHYSICAL HEALTH

Actions
- Exercise
- Set small goals to obtain an end goal
- Maintain daily routine
- Be aware of the physical demands of the profession
- Treat repetitive stress injuries
- Diet
- Proper nutrition

Benefits
- Increased energy levels
- Supports brain function
- Reduced stress
- Improved long-term mobility
- Overall well-being
- Provides body with energy
- Boost immune system

Notes

ETHICS

Principled approach to interpreting

There are many considerations an interpreter must keep in mind while interpreting or accepting/declining an assignment. As interpreters, we must hold ourselves to a high standard, keeping in mind the following points:

- Confidentiality
- Professionalism
- Do no harm
- Social Justice

- **If you are a Mentee in CORE**
  Why did you become an interpreter?

- **If you are a Mentor in CORE**
  What is the role of mentorship in the field of interpreting?
  How have you benefited from mentorship in your career?

- **If you are a Coach in CORE**
  How can you pass down your institutional knowledge to support interpreters and the Deaf community for years to come?

PRIVILEGED ROLE

Maintain confidentiality

Interpreters are in a privileged role and frequently witness intimate moments of people's lives. Therefore, we need to take steps to respect people's privacy.

Be professional

Arriving to assignments on time (i.e. early) is important to building trust with consumers. Interpreters must dress to match the work space and environment. Having an attitude of humility and respect is critical for being a professional interpreter.

Do no harm

To ensure full clarify and comprehension, bring the consumers into your decision making process. Be transparent about your needs and limitations.

Social justice

As an interpreter, you are often working with a minority group who has experienced language deprivation and oppression. Always be aware of equity, advocacy, allyship, and empowerment when interpreting. Learn to follow the lead of the Deaf consumers whenever possible.

AGENCY SCREENINGS

Being a skill based profession, interpreters are typically expected to demonstrate their skills prior to being hired by an interpreting agency or other entity to render services. Screenings are one approach agencies use to determine an interpreter's skill for the types of assignments they commonly provide services for. Many interpreters can feel anxious about this process and while it can be overwhelming, developing a schema for what to expect can be helpful in preparing for a screening appointment.

A typical screening often includes the following tasks:

- Interpreting Spoken English/English Captions to American Sign Language

- Interpreting American Sign Language to Spoken English/English Captions

- Interpreting an interactive dialogue between both American Sign Language to Spoken English/English Captions

- Responding to ethical situational case studies

Questions to consider:

- Where can you find resources to prepare for screenings?

- How should you prepare for screenings?

- Will your screening be done in person or remotely?

- If there is not a screening, does the agency or hiring entity know your skillset?

- Do you know the type of work settings the interpreting agency contracts with?

- How should you decide which agencies to screen with?

- What should you bring with you to a screening?

- What questions should you be prepared to ask or answer during the screening?

SCRIPTS

Many interpreters experience unique situations that require clear and effective communication when explaining their needs and role in specific settings. Below are several common examples of situations interpreters experience in work settings.

Five Common Scenarios

Your Introduction
- Explain the role of a sign language interpreter while emphasizing accessibility
- Explain the difference between simultaneous and consecutive interpreting, which approach you will be using, and the potential for a short time delay
- Emphasize that you will interpret everything, including background or environmental noises and side conversations
- Collaborate with the Deaf consumer in cases where they might prefer to introduce you themselves
- Both the Deaf and hearing persons involved are consumers

Logistics
- Adequate lighting for clear visibility
- Clear sight lines for seating
- Prosody: speak at a normal pace
- Ask the Deaf consumer their preference for interpreter placement, if possible
- Turn-taking in group settings to avoid overlap between participants

Defer to the Deaf Consumer
- Whenever possible, defer questions to the Deaf consumer
- Questions directed at the interpreter about sign language or general side conversations should be and will be interpreted
- How to address common misconceptions about Deaf culture (i.e.: reading lips, hearing impaired, etc)

Interactive Dynamics
- When voicing, you as the interpreter will speak in third person
- Eye contact with the Deaf attendee, interpreter, and hearing participants
- Announce names of speakers on conference calls

Materials
- Requesting prep materials ahead of time
- Educating presenters to allow time for all participants to process visual aids

SCRIPTS

Maintaining confidence in the workplace can be difficult when working and interacting with new people each day. Interpreters who have succinct, well thought out scripts, are able to make more concise, timely, and appropriate ethical decisions. Additionally, they are enabled to explain their roles more effectively to all persons involved.

Scripts can be extremely beneficial when implemented in various interpreting scenarios. In addition to the situations listed above, interpreters often find themselves in a variety of dynamic and unique settings.

Use the space below to brainstorm situations where you may need a script, and then draft a script:

ASSIGNMENT PREPARATION

Preparing for an assignment ahead of time has often been called the key to successful interpreting. As interpreters, especially those who work as freelancers, we frequently move from one new environment to the next without a lot of contextual information. Going into an assignment without preparing, makes it difficult for interpreters to ensure they are making ethical decisions, decisions based on the needs of all consumers and the environmental dynamics.

With this in mind, preparing for assignments should be as much a part of your routine as getting up, getting dressed, and taking care of your other necessities. Being a professional interpreter means we must be ethical in how we approach our work, and preparing for an assignment plays an important role in ethical decision-making.

HOW TO PROPERLY PREPARE
Routine is key

Persons Involved
- What are the clients' language preferences?
- Are you familiar with the clients' background, culture, and identities?
- Do you have any prior work experiences with these clients?

Setting
- Familiarity with the content
- Knowledge of location and logistics
- Situational awareness based on environment

Content
- Request prep from point of contact/schedulers ahead of time
- Ask for names of person(s) involved
- Contact interpreters with experience in that setting as a resource to prepare
- Look into websites and online resources, specifically organizational charts

Team Interpreting
- Do you and your team interpreter have prior experience working together?
- Does your team interpreter have prior experience with that assignment?
- Are you able to pre-conference before the assignment?
- What are your preferences for feedback?
- What teaming dynamics and turn-taking practices do you wish to employ?
- How do you want to communicate during the assignment?
- Will you have the opportunity to debrief after the assignment?

Solo
- Follow up with the agency post-assignment
- Know how to request a Deaf Interpreter
- Know how to request a team interpreter
- Feel confident and able to advocate for yourself
- Be prepared with scripts for managing different assignments
- Know point of contact on-site
- Maintain integrity in the midst of the unknowns

PRO BONO ASSIGNMENTS
Local partnership

Interpreters are granted the unique privilege of being able to work alongside the Deaf community. As part of the CORE Program, and in acknowledgment of this privilege, we make giving back to the local community a priority. Through the provision of pro bono interpreting services in a variety of settings including weddings, family reunions, fundraisers, sporting events, baby showers, birthday parties, and more, Mentees and Mentors show their deep appreciation for the community that has supported their growth.

Pro Bono Requirements

- Complete a minimum of two pro bono assignments during the six-month Program and track hours individually.

- At the conclusion of each Cycle, CORE will request statistics from each Mentee and compile a total hour count. This information will be shared publicly as a cumulative pro bono hour count from the entire Cycle.

- Communicate with their team interpreter on schedules, logistics, prepping, and debriefing.

- Mentees must work with a certified interpreter. If a Mentee is unable to work with their assigned Mentor, the Mentee can ask their Coaches or another certified interpreter to work with them on pro bono assignments.

- Mentees should take the initiative to research, plan, confirm, and prep for pro bono assignments.

- Pro bono assignments can be through official CORE channels or through personal community connections.

- CORE has partnered with several organizations within the local area to provide pro bono services for internal needs. Each of these organizations is aware of the Program and has given us a point of contact (POC). The organizations send requests to our internal CORE POC and we post their requests to a Google Drive Document that is shared with the CORE interpreters in this Cycle. Please contact the organizations directly in order to complete the required minimum of two pro bono assignments during your time with CORE.

- While we do not require the participants in CORE to work with one of these partner organizations, we do suggest these organizations as wonderful potential opportunities to explore, if you are unable to find a pro bono assignment through your own means.

- Mentees should disclose to parties involved that they are an early career interpreter. Additionally, if the Mentee does not have certification, they should disclose this as well.

AMERICANS WITH DISABILITIES ACT

While CORE does support the local community, we also are firm on following the law. Before accepting a pro bono assignment, interpreters involved with CORE should consider the setting and parties involved to determine appropriateness. We encourage all interpreters to look into the Americans with Disabilities Act (ADA) to clarify requirements for businesses or event spaces providing accessibility services.

CALL
TO ACTION

As your Cycle is approaching the end, here are some things to consider and action items to take to capitalize on the Program and continue your professional development. Additionally, CORE has some concrete expectations for Mentees which are outlined below. Remember your career is your own and ultimately, CORE is one short story within your longer story toward working as a professional interpreter. Be patient with yourself as you continue to develop. Interpreters with a professional, humble, and supportive attitude will be more likely to succeed in the field. As an interpreter, you are in a privileged position. Be mindful. You are not entitled to assignments, rather, the role you serve is to share in the broader conversation. Remember your intended purpose and place within the dialogue.

Completing the CORE Program is not the end of your mentorship journey. Look to the generation behind you, and the colleagues that surround you. Step into the role of 'Mentor' for someone else.

Finally, always remember you are part of the CORE Family.

- **If you are a Mentee in CORE**
  After completing the CORE Program, what are your next steps? How can you use this CORE Booklet as a tool in your career?

- **If you are a Mentor in CORE**
  What were some of the lessons learned during this mentorship Cycle? How can you incorporate this CORE Booklet into future Mentor-Mentee relationships?

- **If you are a Coach in CORE**
  Can you identify which Mentors will make strong candidates for Coaches in the future? How can you support them?

NEXT STEPS

Prior to the end of the Cycle, set up a time to meet one-on-one with your Mentor or Mentee. Use this time to discuss what your relationship will look like after the Cycle concludes. Additionally, Mentees can work with their Mentor to create three new goals to begin working on after they are finished with the CORE Program. Mentees should also consider showing appreciation for their Mentor through a simple thank you note or dinner out. Determine with your Mentor if you will continue a working relationship and what boundaries you two will set going forward.

As a group, Mentees, Mentors, and Coaches, will come together for a Completion Event, a celebration of the time spent together developing and growing. This is also an opportunity to discuss the overall mentorship experience, and how you can potentially continue to support one another in the future. While CORE makes an effort to bridge the gaps in the interpreting field, a continuous journey toward connecting the helicopter to the masses, is a longitudinal goal. The experienced interpreters of today, who are in this proverbial helicopter, have to actively throw out a rope to guide and support the next generation. This journey is far from complete. When you are done with your CORE Cycle, we sincerely hope you consider rejoining us in the future to support and extend the rope to those coming after you.

Your CORE Chapter will send out a feedback survey for you to complete prior to exiting the Cycle. Utilize this survey as a way to provide constructive feedback that CORE can use to improve the Program for the next Cycle of interpreters.

INTROSPECTION

Mentors and Mentees, before your formal relationship concludes, set aside some time for self-reflection. During this time, consider how you can improve upon your mentorship and interpreting skills in the future.

Use the following to guide your future development:

STOP DOING

Identify actions or habits you want to work on eliminating from your work or personal life:

START DOING

Identify actions or habits you would
like to try and incorporate into your practice:

KEEP DOING

Recognize actions or habits that are
working for you and serving your career:

CAREER MAPPING

A career map is a tool you can use to outline your goals and ambitions. There are many approaches to creating a career map based on areas of your life you wish to focus. Work alongside your Mentor and Coaches to create a Career Map that reflects the type of interpreter you want to become. Remember to routinely refer to your career map in order to hold yourself accountable in meeting your goals.

Objectives
Set three clear, attainable goals per category, based on an assessment of your current circumstances and your intended outcome.

Personal
Physical health is an important part of your professional interpreting career. While exercise is one aspect of good health, remember that your daily choices and diet also have a major impact on your overall physical well-being.

Mental
We are all human and, as such, experience life stressors. Remember that your personal and professional life are not two separate dichotomies but rather one overlapping synergy or relationships and values. Being able to prioritize your personal needs is necessary for your overall sense of well-being.

Budget

Understanding and organizing your finances can have a positive impact on your overall stress levels. By managing and monitoring your finances you can feel confident in your ability to live within your means. When budgeting, include retirement, insurance, and an emergency fund as individual line items. Many interpreters who are starting off their career are not quite ready to work full-time, so remember that part-time work may be necessary as you gain the skill set for full-time interpreting.

Updates

Remember to create deadlines for your goals and to consistently check in on them. In doing so, you hold yourself accountable for your own career and maintain self-motivation. Working alongside a Mentor can also provide another level of accountability. Additionally, a Mentor can support your development in ensuring your goals are ethically sound.

Appearance

Make a career map unique to you and aligned with your needs. Some people are more numbers oriented, while others are more visual. Your career map should capture your personality and be a reflection of who you are and who you want to become.

Alterations

Life does not always happen in tandem with your goals. Even with a clear structure, defined categories, and specific objectives, your career map may need adjustments as time passes.

CORE has Career Map Templates for you to utilize on our CORE website under the CORE Resource Library (CRL). However, keep in mind that these are not the only options. We encourage you to create a career map that uniquely reflects you. The main goal of those templates in the CRL is to provide a starting point for you to build on in the coming weeks, months, and years.

Questions to consider when creating your career map:

Past

- Who supported your personal and professional development?

- How did they make you feel and how did they create a safe environment?

Present

- What impact do you have within the Deaf community?

- What is an ally and how can you be an ally?

- Who are the current key players in the interpreting field?

Future

- What kind of interpreting career do you want to make for yourself?

- Who are the future key players in the interpreting field?

- How can you continuously give back to the Deaf community?

- How can you support expanding diversity in the interpreting field?

- What should the interpreting field look like in thirty years?

- How can you maintain balance between your work and personal lives?

- What is an ally and how can you be an ally?

INTERPRETERS SUPPORTING INTERPRETERS

CORE is a Program in search of a cultural shift in the field of interpreting. Through our work, we want to see more interpreters learn to incorporate the humanity aspect of the field - learning from colleagues and supporting each other on their own journeys of growth and development. We want to encourage all interpreters to approach our work in an intentional, and mindful manner by incorporating all of the skills in our toolkit. As a service oriented field, we must never forget that our moments on the job can leave lifelong impacts on the people we are privileged to work with.

This Program is a microcosm of the wider interpreting field. Through CORE, we seek to foster a sense of community and collaboration both within each Cycle and beyond. Just as Coaches support Mentors and both support Mentees, we hope all participants who take part in CORE carry with them a sense of accountability and community. As interpreters proceed throughout their career, it is important for them to always remember those who lifted them up and strive to do the same for others.

May we never stop
DEVELOPING
LEARNING
MENTORING

Made in the USA
Middletown, DE
05 November 2020